CONTENTS

WHO WERE THE GREEKS?

Greece is a country in the south of Europe. It is warm and sunny and is almost completely surrounded by sea. There are many rugged mountains. They run across the land in long lines, called ranges.

Because much of Greece is covered in mountains, the Greeks have always lived by the sea, where the land is flatter and easier to farm.

THE ANCIENT GREEKS

JOHN MALAM

WAYLAND

HISTORY STARTS HERE!
The Ancient Greeks
OTHER TITLES IN THE SERIES
The Ancient Egyptians • The Ancient Romans
• The Tudors •

Produced for Wayland Publishers Limited by
Roger Coote Publishing
Gissing's Farm
Fressingfield
Suffolk IP21 5SH
England

Designer: Victoria Webb
Cover design: Paul Cherill
Editor: Alex Edmonds
Illustrations: Michael Posen

First published in Great Britain in 1999 by Wayland Publishers Ltd

Reprinted in 2000 by Wayland,
An imprint of Hachette Children's Books

Paperback edition published in 2003 by Wayland
This edition published in 2008 by Wayland

Wayland
338 Euston Road
London NW1 3BH

British Library Cataloguing in Publication Data
Malam, John
  The ancient Greeks. – (History starts here)
  1.Greece – History – To 146 BC. – Juvenile literature
  2.Greece – Civilization – To 146 BC. – Juvenile literature
  I.Title
  938

ISBN: 978-0-7502-5392-5

Printed and bound in China

Front cover picture: A Greek vase.
Title page picture: A vase showing women making offerings to the gods.
Picture acknowledgements:AKG London Ltd: 6, 10, 14 (Erich Lessing), 15 (Alfons Rath),
22 (John Hios), 27 (Erich Lessing); Ancient Art and Architecture Collection 18 (R Sheridan),
23 (R Sheridan), 29 (M&J Lynch); British Museum 1, 17; CM Dixon: 7, 8, 13, 19, 21, 24,
25, 26, 28; ET Archive: front cover; Tony Stone Images: 4 (George Grigoriou),
9 (Mervyn Rees), 10–11 (George Grigoriou), 20 (Robert Everts).
Every attempt has been made to clear copyright for this edition. Should there be any inadvertent
omission please apply to the publisher for rectification.

Wayland is a division of Hachette Children's Books, an Hachette Livre UK company

BULGARIA
MACEDONIA
ALBANIA
Mount
Olympus
GREECE
Ionian
Sea
Aegean
Sea
TURKEY
Delphi
Athens
Mycenae
Olympia
Epidaurus
Mediterranean
Sea
Knossos
CRETE

This map shows how the mainland part of Greece is joined to other countries in Europe. About 2,000 islands belong to Greece. Less than 200 of them have people living on them.

It was here, more than 2,000 years ago, that the ancient Greeks lived. They created one of the world's first important civilizations. Some of the things we have today, such as the alphabet, the theatre and the Olympic Games were started all those years ago by the ancient Greeks.

THE BEGINNING OF GREECE

The Minoans and the Mycenaeans were the first two important groups of people in Greece.

The Minoans lived on Crete and other islands nearby. They built palaces with many rooms. They farmed the land and fished and hunted. They also knew how to write. The Minoans had their own language, which was not Greek.

This Minoan picture shows people leaping over the back of a charging bull. This was a game that young Minoan men played.

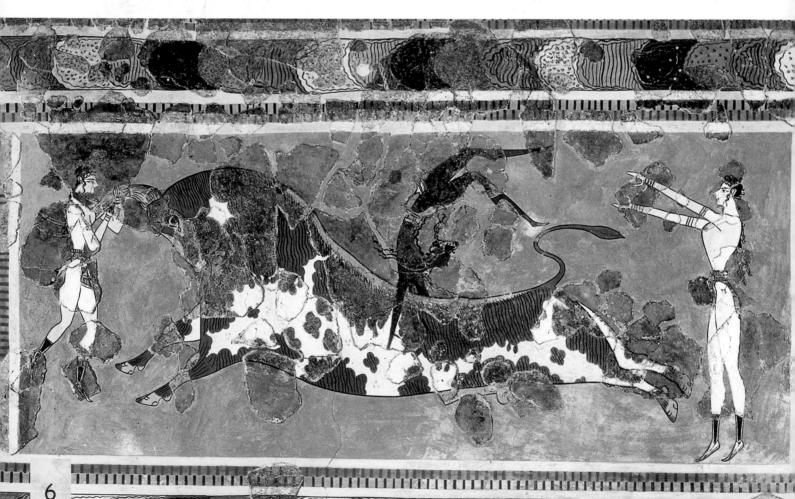

The city of Mycenae was built on top of a hill. Its strong walls protected the town from attackers.

A MYSTERIOUS END

Nobody knows how these two civilizations came to an end. Some people think that the great palaces of Minos were destroyed by a volcano erupting. Mycenae is thought to have disappeared because its people were at war with each other.

The Mycenaeans lived on the mainland. They lived in towns around the city of Mycenae and were ruled over by kings. The Mycenaeans spoke a type of Greek. They are said to be the first Greeks.

The Minoans and the Mycenaeans lived about 4,000 years ago and they traded with each other. The idea of writing spread from the Minoans to the Mycenaeans. Then, about 3,000 years ago, both civilizations came to an end.

ATHENS - CITY OF MARBLE

The Greeks who lived after the Mycenaeans built many towns and cities. One city, called Athens, became more powerful than all the rest.

Athens was at its most powerful 2,500 years ago. It was a busy city. As many as 200,000 people lived there and in the countryside around. Athens owned valuable silver mines, and, like other Greek cities, had its own army. It had a fleet of warships, too.

Pericles was a great leader in Athens. He ordered the Parthenon to be built.

On top of a high hill stood a group of beautiful temples. They were built from marble, which is a hard white stone. The grandest temple of all was the Parthenon.

The Parthenon was once painted in bright colours, but the paint has worn away. It was built to honour the goddess Athena.

HOW A CITY WAS RUN

The ancient Greeks invented a form of government called 'democracy'. This means 'power by the people'. It was a fair system because the citizens of Greece could decide how they wanted their city to be run.

An unpopular man could be sent away from the city if the citizens of Athens voted for him to go. They voted on pieces of broken pottery, called *Ostraka*.

In Athens, citizens held their meetings in the open air on the Pnyx hill. Its name meant 'packing place'.

Greek citizens chose their own leaders, made laws, and decided whether to go to war or not. Citizens were men born in the city, whose parents had been born there, too. It did not matter if they were rich or poor.

GREEK CITIZENS

Only some people were allowed to be citizens of the city where they lived. Women, slaves and outsiders from other Greek cities or foreign lands, could not be citizens.

LIFE IN ANCIENT GREECE

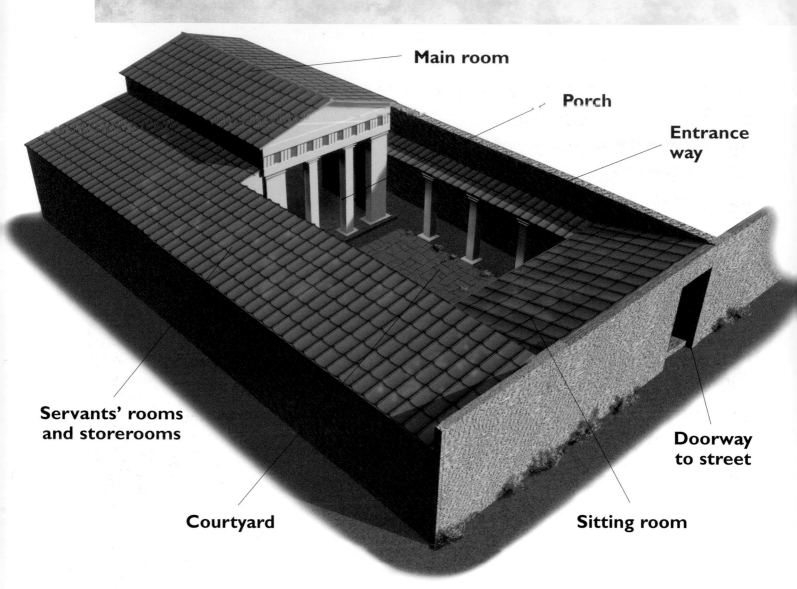

Main room

Porch

Entrance way

Servants' rooms and storerooms

Doorway to street

Courtyard

Sitting room

This is how a Greek house might have looked. Everyday life centred around the courtyard. This was where children played, where food was cooked, and where visitors were met.

People lived in houses built from bricks of clay. Walls were painted white to keep the heat of the Sun out. Houses had several rooms, placed around a courtyard. There were separate rooms for women, men, guests and slaves. The main room was for feasting and entertaining guests.

A woman was expected to stay at home and look after the household. She cooked, cleaned and cared for the children. She made the family's clothes. If the family had slaves, she gave them orders.

Men were free to come and go from the house as they wished. They went to work, bought food in the market square and visited temples and festivals.

This woman is spinning wool to make cloth.

13

CHILDREN AND SCHOOL

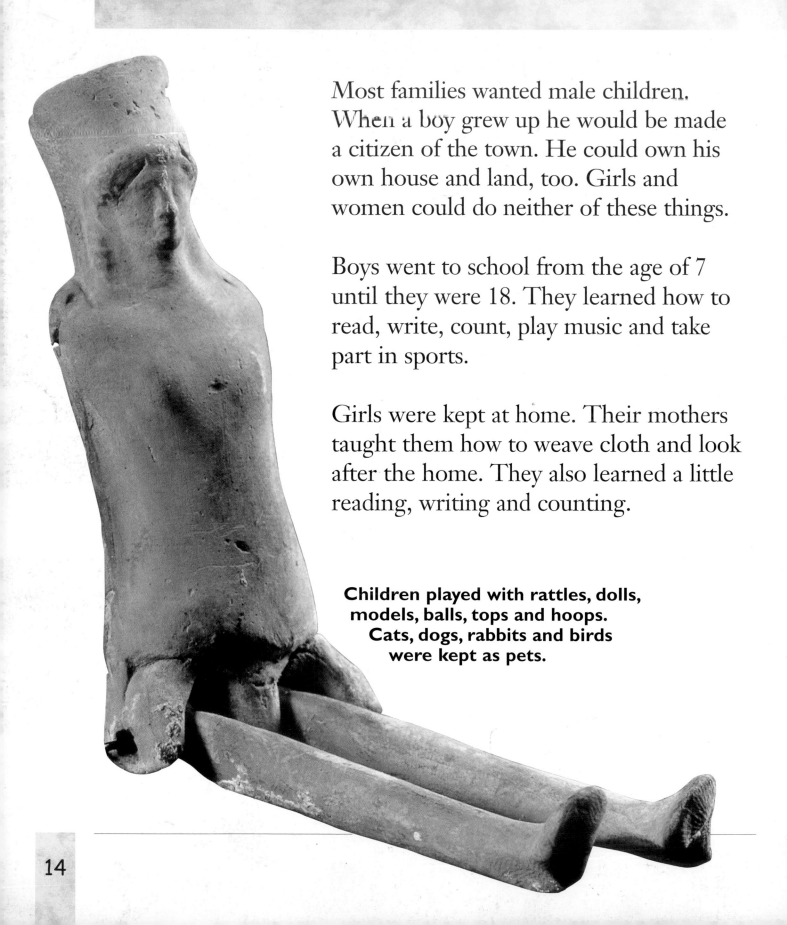

Most families wanted male children. When a boy grew up he would be made a citizen of the town. He could own his own house and land, too. Girls and women could do neither of these things.

Boys went to school from the age of 7 until they were 18. They learned how to read, write, count, play music and take part in sports.

Girls were kept at home. Their mothers taught them how to weave cloth and look after the home. They also learned a little reading, writing and counting.

Children played with rattles, dolls, models, balls, tops and hoops. Cats, dogs, rabbits and birds were kept as pets.

14

There were 24 letters in the Greek alphabet. The word 'alphabet' comes from the names of the first two Greek letters, *alpha* and *beta*.

GREEK CLOTHES

Warm clothes were woven from sheeps' wool. The flax plant was used to make linen, which was thinner and lighter than wool.

A man dressed for travelling. He wears a short cloak, a hat to keep the sun off his head, and leather walking boots with laces.

DYES

Clothes were usually left a natural creamy-white colour. Sometimes dyes were used. Yellow dye was made from part of the crocus flower. Red came from the leaves of the madder plant. Purple came from the crushed shells of sea snails.

Because a lot of cloth was used in Greek clothes, they hung in neat, loose folds from the shoulders and waist.

Most Greek clothes were made from rectangular-shaped material. The material was draped around the body and pins, brooches and belts fastened it in place. Men, women and children wore similar styles of clothing.

Most people had short hair. If a woman had long hair, she might tie it up with ribbons.

FOOD AND DRINK

Bread, biscuits and porridge were the main foods eaten by everyone. They were all made from barley, which grew in Greece.

FEASTING

One of the dishes enjoyed by Greek men at dinner parties was roast pig stuffed with thrushes, ducks, eggs, and oysters! That was washed down with scented wine to drink, and then followed by fruit, nuts and cake.

This painting on a vase shows olives being knocked from a tree with sticks. Oil was squeezed from olives, which grew well in Greece. It was used in cooking, and in lamps where it was burned to give light.

18

Farmers grew vegetables in their fields and sold them in the town's market square. They grew beans, peas, lentils, cabbages, cucumbers, lettuces, leeks, onions and garlic. They gathered walnuts, chestnuts and hazelnuts. Fruit crops were apples, pears, olives, grapes, dates and figs.

The Greeks ate meat from sheep, pigs, cattle and birds, as well as fish.

Most feasts were for men only. They ate and drank in the main room of the house, while lying on couches.

GODS AND GODDESSES

The ancient Greeks had many gods. Because people wanted the gods to protect and help them, they gave them presents. Some gave gifts of food and wine. The greatest gift was an animal, such as a sheep or a goat. It was killed by a priest, and prayers were spoken.

People thought their wishes would be granted if the gifts pleased the gods. Farmers prayed for good harvests. Travellers prayed for safe journeys and the sick prayed for good health.

The Greeks built great Temples to please their gods. People from all over Greece went to this temple at Delphi to pray to Apollo, the god of healing.

This is Poseidon, the god of the sea. Statues often show him holding a three-pronged fish spear, called a trident.

Poseidon was a brother of Zeus, the king of the gods. Zeus was the god of weather. Statues often show him throwing a thunder bolt.

FESTIVALS AND GAMES

At a festival, people relaxed and enjoyed themselves. It was time to celebrate and give thanks to the gods. Colourful processions were held.

Sports festivals were always popular. The greatest of all was the Olympic Games. This took place once every four years at Olympia. The festival lasted five days.

It was at the racetrack in Olympia that most of the events took place. The pentathlon was a mix of five different athletic events that each competitor had to enter.

Athletes in ancient Greece did not wear clothes. The paintings on this vase show athletes being presented with prizes at the games.

Men from all parts of Greece, and from overseas too, went to Olympia to take part in the games. Women were not allowed to go there. A winning athlete was given a crown of olive branches. He brought honour to his city by winning at the games.

STORIES AND THEATRE

Stories were a part of everyday life in Greece. Storytellers, or bards, learned stories by heart, then told them from memory. Crowds gathered to listen.

Homer was a poet who told many popular stories. He might have been blind, which is why he is shown with his eyes shut.

You can see from this theatre at Epidaurus how the audience sat in the open air on stone seats. Plays were performed in the daytime.

People liked to go to the theatre. Actors wore masks and costumes, and put on lots of different plays. All the actors were men. Some plays were funny and some were serious. They were set in the past and told stories about gods and heroes.

THE GREEKS AT WAR

The ancient Greeks fought many battles. Greek cities argued and fought wars with each other as well as with other countries.

The Greeks went to war with the Persians, who wanted to invade Athens. The Athenians were led by a great commander, Themistocles. At Salamis they fought a great sea battle. The Persians were beaten and they lost 400 ships.

Greek warships had battering rams. They smashed into enemy ships and made big holes in their wooden sides to sink them.

Greek soldiers fought with swords and long spears. They wore armour to protect their bodies.

THE END OF THE GREEKS

The most famous Greek soldier was Alexander. Under his leadership, the Greeks controlled land from Greece to India. After Alexander the Great died, his empire was split up into smaller parts. Greece became less powerful.

Many years later, the Romans came from Italy, to the west of Greece. They built a powerful empire of their own. Greece became part of it.

Alexander was a hero. Because he was such a great leader, he became known as Alexander the Great.

This is a temple which the Romans built in France. It was copied from the style of temples the Greeks built.

The ancient Greeks have taught us many things. Their influence can still be seen today in our art, our sport and the way our countries are governed.

THE ROMANS

The Romans liked the Greeks and the way they lived. They admired the style of their buildings, which they copied, and they based their alphabet on the Greek alphabet. They also enjoyed Greek plays and poetry.

IMPORTANT DATES

All the dates in this list are 'BC' dates. This stands for 'Before Christ'. BC dates are counted back from the year 0, which is the year we say Jesus Christ was born. Some dates have the letter 'c.' in front of them. This stands for 'circa', which means 'about'. These dates are guesses, because no one knows what the real date is.

2000 BC The very first Greek-speaking people arrived in mainland Greece.

c.2000 BC The Minoans built palaces on Crete.

c.1900 BC The Mycenaeans built towns on mainland Greece.

1600 BC Mycenae flourishes.

c.1400 BC The first Greek writing was made. The town of Mycenae was at its greatest.

c.1200 BC The traditional date of the Trojan War.

c.1100 BC The Minoan and Mycenaean civilizations came to an end.

800–500 BC The Archaic Period. The time when ancient Greece began to expand and grow rich.

c.800 BC The Greeks make their own language.

c.800 BC Homer, the greatest Greek poet, lived.

776 BC The first Olympic Games were held.

753 BC Rome was founded.

753 BC Greek poetry became very famous.

500–336 BC The Classical Age. The period when Athens went to war with the Persians and Pericles was leader of Athens.

534 BC The first Greek tragedy was performed.

c.500 BC Democracy was introduced in Athens.

490 BC The Greeks beat the Persians in a battle on land.

480 BC The Greeks beat the Persians in a battle at sea.

479–431 BC The Golden Age. The period when Athens became a wealthy and popular city.

447–438 BC The Parthenon was built in Athens.

431–404 BC Athens lost a war with Sparta, another city in Greece.

430 BC Plague in Athens.

359–336 BC The reign of King Philip II.

338 BC King Philip II conquered and became the ruler of Greece.

336 BC King Philip II died. His son, Alexander, took over from him.

327 BC Alexander's army conquered the Persian army.

323 BC Alexander died, and his empire broke up.

146 BC Greece became part of the Roman Empire.

GLOSSARY

Bard Another name for a storyteller.
Citizen A Greek who was born a free man, and who had a say in how he wanted his town to be run.
Democracy A type of government in which ordinary people have a say in how they want things to be done.
Marble A hard white stone.
Minoans A group of people who lived on Crete and other islands nearby.
Mount Olympus A mountain in the north of Greece where the gods lived.
Mycenaeans A group of people who lived mostly on the mainland of Greece.

Olympians The name given to the family of twelve major gods and goddesses.
Olympic Games The most important festival of sport.
Persians People who lived in Persia, now called Iran.
Poseidon The god of the sea.
Servant Someone who works for another person.
Slave Someone who is owned by another person.
Zeus The king of the gods. He was the god of the weather.

FURTHER INFORMATION

BOOKS TO READ
Ancient Greece by Andrew Solway (Oxford University Press, 2001)
Men, Women and Children in Ancient Rome by Colin Hynson (Wayland, 2007)

All About Ancient Greece by Anna Claybourne (Wayland, 2002)
Gods & Goddesses: In the Daily Life of the Ancient Greeks by Fiona MacDonald (Wayland, 2002)

Find Out About Ancient Greece by Colin Hynson (Wayland, 2007)
Ancient Greece by Anne Pearson (Dorling Kindersley Eyewitness Guides, 1992)

INDEX

A Land of Mystery

Ancient Egypt has always amazed people. It was a land of hidden tombs, golden treasures and scary animal gods. But what were the people who lived there really like?

Today, we know a lot from the things found in their tombs. We can also read their writing. But there is still something special about the Ancient Egyptians (say "ee-jip-shans").

People are often a bit scared by mummies. They still wonder at the great pyramids built 5,000 years ago. If you'd like to know more about the amazing Egyptians, read on!

Egyptian patterns are still very popular. They were even used on the famous ship *Titanic*.

People of the Nile

The Nile is the longest river in the world, but the Ancient Egyptians just called it "the river". It gave them all their water and food.

When the Nile flooded each year, the waters covered the desert with black mud. To the Egyptians, the mud was a gift from the gods. Without it, they couldn't grow their crops.

READING ABOUT

Ancient
Egyptians

David Jay

Contents

This edition published in 2003

© Aladdin Books Ltd 2000

Designed and produced by
Aladdin Books Ltd
28 Percy Street
London W1T 2BZ

First published in
Great Britain in 2000 by
Franklin Watts
96 Leonard Street
London EC2A 4XD

ISBN 0 7496 5087 7

Printed in U.A.E.

Editor: Jim Pipe

Historical Consultant
Dominic Montserrat

Series Literacy Consultant
Wendy Cobb

Design
Flick, Book Design and Graphics

Picture Research
Brooks Krikler Research

A catalogue record for this book is
available from the British Library.

The Ancient Egyptians planned their lives around the flood. Their year was divided into the flood season, the growing season and the dry season.

In the growing season, farmers made animals push seeds into the mud with their feet.

In the dry season, the farmers built ditches. These carried the Nile waters across the land and helped the farmers to grow more food.

Most Egyptians lived along the Nile. Few people lived anywhere else because it was just desert.

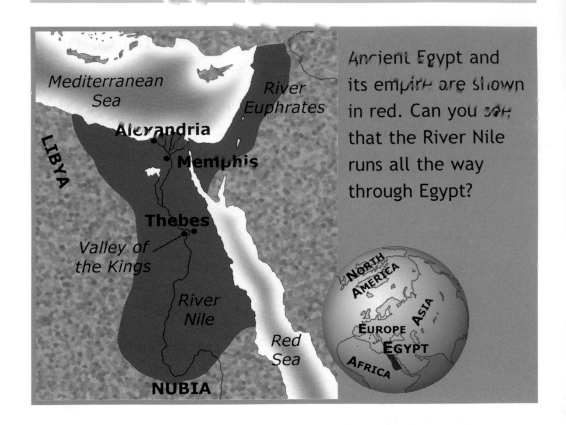

Mediterranean Sea

River Euphrates

Alexandria

Memphis

LIBYA

Thebes

Valley of the Kings

River Nile

Red Sea

NUBIA

Ancient Egypt and its empire are shown in red. Can you see that the River Nile runs all the way through Egypt?

NORTH AMERICA

ASIA

EUROPE

EGYPT

AFRICA

The Egyptians had to work together to build the ditches. So they created a strong leader. He was called a pharaoh (say "fair-row"), or king.

When one pharaoh died, one of his family became king. Some families ruled for hundreds of years. The Nile helped the pharaohs build a strong country — Ancient Egypt lasted for over 3,000 years.

The pharaohs and the people were proud of what they did. That's why they left behind thousands of pictures of themselves, covered with lots of carved writing.

In the end, the Ancient Greeks took over Egypt. Later, the Romans shut down all the temples and kicked out the priests — the last people who could read Egyptian writing.

For over 1,500 years, no one could read this ancient writing. The secrets of Ancient Egypt were lost to the world.

Egyptians wrote with pictures. But what did they mean?

Digging Up Egypt

Collectors explored inside the pyramids.

Nearly 200 years ago, the French emperor Napoleon attacked Egypt. He brought Egyptian experts as well as soldiers to the area.

One day, they found a black stone with three kinds of writing on it — two kinds of the Egyptian language and one in Ancient Greek.

After 14 years, a clever young French man, called Champollion, worked out how to read Egyptian writing. Now people could find out what the Ancient Egyptians were saying.

Collectors took objects from Ancient Egypt back to museums. Then came archaeologists (say "ar-key-yollo-jists"), people who study the past by digging up ancient things.

Their greatest find was the tomb (the burial place) of the boy king Tutankhamun (say "too-tan-car-moon").

Seventy years ago, an English team started to dig for it. The team was led by Howard Carter.

Tutankhamun's gold mask weighs over 10 kg.

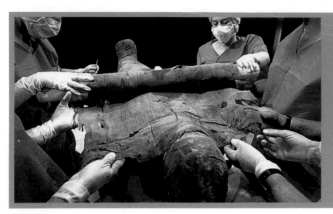

When pharaohs died, their bodies were wrapped in bandages. We call these bodies "mummies".

After two days, a boy found a step beneath the sand. Soon they had opened up a room. Here, Carter saw "strange animals, statues and gold — everywhere the glint of gold".

Finds like this helped to tell us what the Ancient Egyptians were like. It's lucky for us that the Egyptians buried so much with them when they died.

The Egyptians built wonderful furniture out of wood. Many pieces survived in hidden tombs.

Egyptian People

Pharaohs • Scribes • Craft Workers • Women

A pharaoh was very powerful. To Egyptians, he was both a god and a human. He could speak to other gods and make the floods happen. Most people could only talk to the gods using priests.

Women didn't usually become pharaohs. Queen Hatshepsut was a female pharaoh, but she was shown in pictures wearing a beard and was called "His Majesty".

A pharaoh had one main queen and a few minor ones. Some pharaohs married their sisters.

Queen Hatshepsut's temple is still one of the most beautiful buildings in the world.

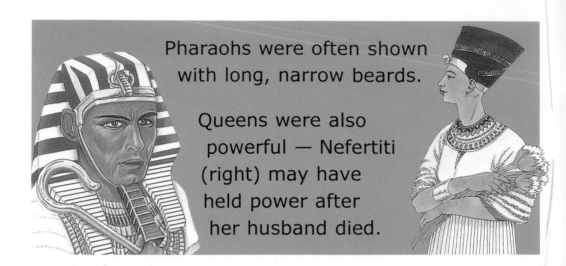

Pharaohs were often shown with long, narrow beards.

Queens were also powerful — Nefertiti (right) may have held power after her husband died.

The pharaohs also had concubines. Concubines were like wives but they weren't as important. The pharaoh Ramses II was said to have had a hundred concubines and a hundred children.

The best jobs, like those of priests, generals and ministers, went to the pharaoh's family or clever people chosen by the pharaohs.

Scribes (people who could write) could get good jobs. Good jobs were collecting the taxes, running building sites or making sure the army had all the things it needed.

Next down came the craft workers. They did beautiful work in stone, metal, wood and clay. They made furniture, pots, wall-carvings and jewellery which are still in style today.

There were no lawyers in Ancient Egypt. In court, people had to defend themselves.

Bottom of the pile were the farm workers. They also worked as builders on the huge temples and pyramids. People were paid in cloth or food (usually bread or beer).

Rich Egyptians had a few slaves to help them in the house and on farms. They also used dogs for hunting. Some even trained baboons to pick fruit from the trees.

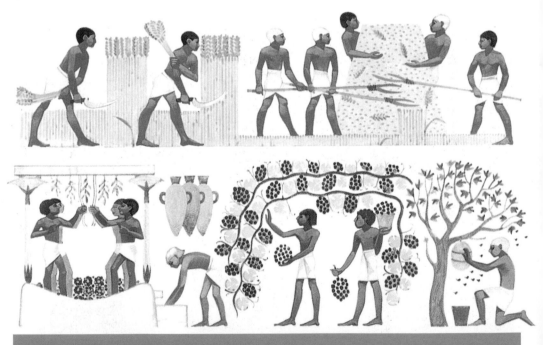

Egyptian wall paintings show us how they worked. What is happening here? Answer on page 32.

Women ran the homes, helped on the farms and did weaving by hand. Some women also worked as singers and dancers.

Women in Ancient Egypt could also own land and leave their husband if they wanted to. This was more than women in most modern countries could do just a hundred years ago.

This woman shows how the Egyptians ground grain to make flour, like the ancient statue below.

Egypt at War

Upper and Lower Egypt • Armies • Explorers

The Egyptians were not very interested in fighting. But from time to time, Egypt went to war. It also fought with itself. At first there were two Egypts — Upper Egypt to the south and Lower Egypt to the north.

Menes' crown

Under pharaoh Menes, the two Egypts became one. Menes wore a double crown, a white one for Upper Egypt and a red one for Lower Egypt.

Egyptian soldiers fought with bows and small axes.

The Egyptians also sailed north up the Nile into the Mediterranean Sea. They called it "the Great Green". Traders also sailed nearly all the way down the east coast of Africa.

Later, Egypt fought with Libya to the west and Nubia to the south (can you find these on page 6?). At times they ruled Nubia. They even ruled over land as far away as the River Euphrates in Asia.

Later pharaohs fought in chariots. Most chariots had two people in them. Why? The answer is on page 32.

17

Daily Life

Egyptian houses were made of mud brick, with wooden roofs covered with plaster and palm branches. Most houses had just one or two rooms, but rich people had large villas.

Houses had very thick walls and small, high windows to keep the sun out. This kept the houses cool.

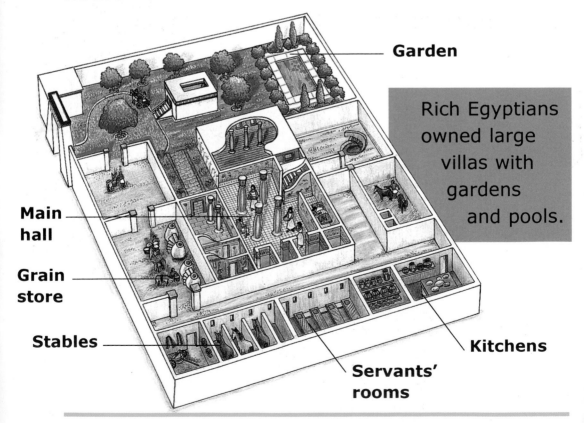

Garden

Main hall

Grain store

Stables

Servants' rooms

Kitchens

Rich Egyptians owned large villas with gardens and pools.

Wooden head rests, used like a pillow, were among the few items in most Egyptian homes.

Though the rich often had beautiful furniture, most people only had a few wooden stools and chests to store their things in.

In towns, the houses were often narrow and tall. The streets were dusty, noisy and crowded.

Craft workers lived in simple houses like these.

Here market stalls sold everything from cloth and animals to pots and pans. There was no money so people just swapped goods.

Food was often cooked outside the house using sticks and animal dung as fuel. It was probably quite tasty.

Farms provided fruit and vegetables as well as meat, milk and cheese. People also fished in the Nile and hunted wild animals and birds.

Rich Egyptians loved parties. At a feast there might be musicians, jugglers and dancers.

The Egyptians enjoyed sweet pastries and cakes. They also had at least a dozen different types of beer (which was as thick as porridge).

Most of the time, women wore white linen dresses, often tight-fitting and with folds in the cloth. Men wore short skirts around their waists.

Egypt's women loved make-up and jewellery. They wore black eye-liner to make their eyes seem larger. Egyptian women liked to keep very clean and used special soap and oils.

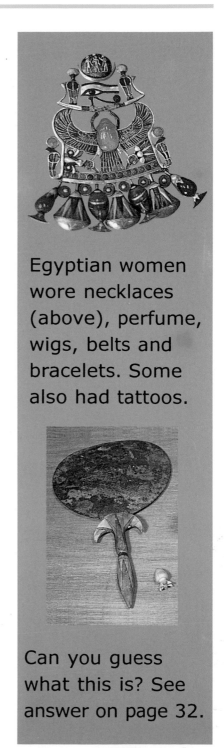

Egyptian women wore necklaces (above), perfume, wigs, belts and bracelets. Some also had tattoos.

Can you guess what this is? See answer on page 32.

Some people shaved their heads to keep cool. Others had long hair with beads or curls. Children had shaved heads — except for a single lock.

Only rich boys went to scribe school. Other boys worked in the fields or learned a trade. Girls helped at home. Children often had animal names, such as "Frog", "Monkey" or "Hippo".

Pens

Coloured inks

Writing was a special skill in Ancient Egypt. Only scribes could read the picture writing in temples and tombs.

Gods and Tombs

Gods • Temples • Pyramids • Tombs • Mummies

Religion was very important to the Ancient Egyptians. Every part of their lives was ruled by a different god. If they wanted happiness, they prayed to the cat goddess Bastet. If they were ill, they might pray to the god Anubis.

Amon Re, Sun god	Sobek, God of Water	Isis, Goddess of Women	Bastet, Goddess of Happiness

The Egyptians drew many of their gods with animal heads and human bodies. The type of animal showed what sort of god it was. Sobek, who was the god of water, had the head of a crocodile (which lives in a river).

Most Egyptians prayed at home and at holy places outside. Every town also had a temple where priests prayed to the gods.

The most important link to the gods was the pharaoh. The Egyptians believed that he was the son of the sun god, Amon Re.

Only the pharaoh could make the sun rise each day, and only he could make the waters of the River Nile flood the land.

Each god, including the pharaohs, had a temple. The Great Temple of Amon Re, near Thebes, was used for 2,000 years. Another amazing building was the temple at Abu Simbel (shown in this picture).

The Great Pyramid at Giza was made of 2.6 million blocks of stone. It took 23 years to build.

Because the pharaoh was so important, the Egyptians wanted him to carry on helping them after he died. They built tombs and filled them with all the things the pharaoh would need in the next world.

So pharaohs had not only temples but huge tombs where they were buried. The most famous tombs are the pyramids.

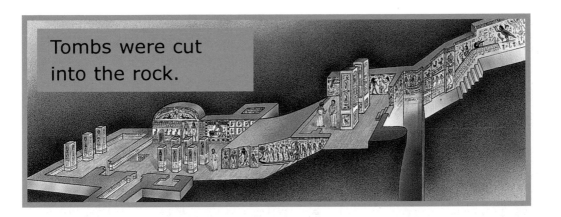

Tombs were cut into the rock.

Because of robbers, later pharaohs had their tombs cut into cliffs. Many of these tombs were built in the famous Valley of the Kings (see map on page 6). But robbers still found many of the secret tombs.

Egyptians also believed in all kinds of magic. They carried charms and used spells.

The Egyptians thought that when they died they would go to a better world.

Magic charms protected against illness and bad luck.

The Ancient Egyptians wanted to keep the
dead bodies in good shape for the next world.
That's why they turned dead people and
animals into mummies.

Priests took out the insides, dried the bodies
and wrapped them in hundreds of metres of
cloth soaked in a sort of glue.

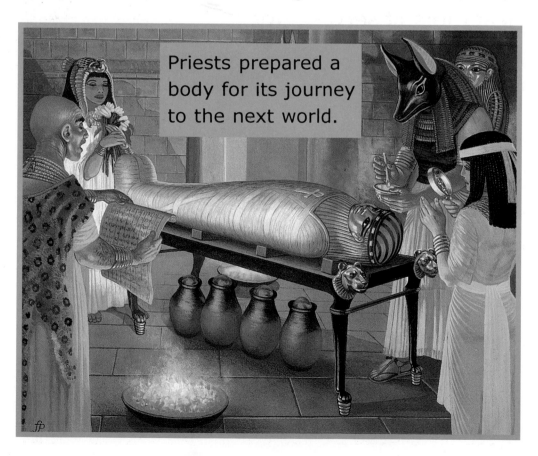

Priests prepared a body for its journey to the next world.

Canopic jars

The priests stored the inside parts of the body in special jars, called canopic jars.

The dead took with them everything they needed for their journey. For a pharaoh, this meant lots of servants (or models of them), food, clothes and furniture.

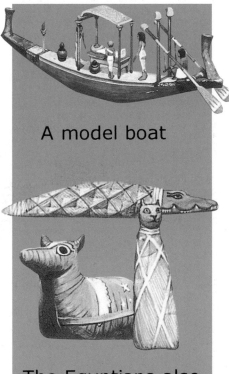

A model boat

Tutankhamun took with him 30 types of wine, 100 shoes, 30 boomerangs and the world's first sofa bed.

Mummies and other objects tell us a lot about how the Ancient Egyptians lived. But there are many other mysteries still to be solved!

The Egyptians also buried mummies of cats, dogs and even crocodiles!

Find Out More

We know a lot about the Egyptians from their tombs. Can you name five things you might find in an Egyptian tomb? Below are a few pictures from the book, which should give you some clues. The answers are on page 32.

UNUSUAL WORDS

Here we explain some words you may have read in this book.

Archaeologist (ar-key-yollo-gist) Someone who discovers things about the past by digging up the ground to look for old buildings or objects.

Canopic jars Priests put the inside parts of a mummy into these special jars.

Mummy A dead body wrapped in bandages and stuffed with chemicals to make it last. The word "mummy" means tar in Arabic, as people once thought that mummies were covered in tar.

Pharaoh The Egyptian king. To the Ancient Egyptians, the pharaoh was also a god, the son of the sun god Amon Re.

Pyramid A building with four triangular sides that meet in a point at the top. The first pyramids were built in steps. Later, the Egyptians built pyramids with smooth sides.

Scribes People who had been taught to write. They often got good jobs in Ancient Egypt.

Temple A building where the priests prayed to the gods.

Tomb A special building where dead bodies are buried. Some tombs are above the ground, others are cut into the rock.

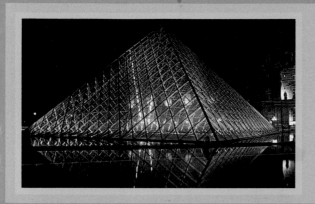

Popular Pyramids

The pyramid shape of the Ancient Egyptians is still very popular. This glass pyramid is part of the famous Louvre Museum in Paris, France.

FAMOUS EGYPTIANS

Cleopatra

Perhaps the most famous Egyptian pharaoh was the last — Cleopatra, a Greek (below). She was known for her great intelligence and charm. She tried to use this to stop Rome from taking over Egypt — but failed.

Ramses II

This pharaoh (left) was a great soldier and builder. He died when he was 90, after reigning for 67 years.

Khufu

This early pharaoh built the Great Pyramid at Giza about 5,000 years ago. He was buried with a whole ship.

Who Came First?

Egyptians	Greeks	Romans	Vikings	Present Day
4,000 years ago	2,500 years ago	2,000 years ago	1,000 years ago	Now

Index

ANSWERS TO PICTURE QUESTIONS

Page 14 The workers above are harvesting grain. The workers below are collecting grapes and crushing them to make wine. The man on the right is collecting honey.
Page 17 It took one man to drive the chariot, and one man to fight.
Page 21 It's a bronze mirror.

Page 30 The things you might find in an Egyptian tomb are: golden mask, human mummy, animal mummies (such as cats, birds and crocodiles), furniture (such as chairs, beds and tables), models of servants, food and wine, clothes and shoes, and models of ships.

Illustrators: Pete Roberts – Allied Artists, Stephen Sweet – SGA; Gerald Wood, Ivan Lapper, Mike Lacey, Peter Kesteven and Dave Burroughs. **Photocredits:** *Abbreviations: t-top, m-middle, b-bottom, r-right, l-left, c-centre.* Cover - Digital Stock; 1, 5, 7, 9, 21r & 26 – Spectrum Colour Library; 15 – Eye Ubiquitous; 11 & 31 – Frank Spooner Pictures.